The Palace of Holyroodhouse

OFFICIAL SOUVENIR

Contents

The Forecourt is dominated by the fountain erected as part of Queen Victoria's improvements to the palace. Intricately carved with sixteenth-century figures, it is based on James V's fountain at Linlithgow Palace.

Introduction

'**HOLYROOD IS A HOUSE** of many memories', wrote Robert Louis Stevenson in 1878. With a history dating back over 500 years, the Palace of Holyroodhouse has been the setting for royal marriages that have changed the course of history for both Scotland and England, and has witnessed treachery, rebellion – and even murder.

As the official residence of Her Majesty The Queen in Scotland, Holyroodhouse is a working palace. When The Queen is in residence during Royal Week, she carries out a wide range of public engagements, ranging from private audiences with politicians and visiting dignitaries to receptions and investitures. On occasion, state visits are held at the palace, and the State Apartments are also used by other members of the Royal Family throughout the year to host events for Scottish organisations with which they are associated.

At other times the palace is open to the public. The exterior today stands virtually unchanged since it was rebuilt for Charles II in the seventeenth century. Inside, visitors follow the processional route through the State Apartments that were designed for the king and intended to impress all who entered with the majesty of his restored monarchy, before climbing the spiral staircase to the rooms where Mary, Queen of Scots lived, and which still retain the atmosphere of those turbulent days.

RIGHT
The processional route through the King's Apartments, looking from the Privy Chamber to the Great Gallery.

OVERLEAF
The Palace of Holyroodhouse from Arthur's Seat, with the Firth of Forth in the distance.

BELOW LEFT
Detail of carving in the ruins of Holyrood Abbey.

BELOW RIGHT
The Privy Chamber looks out over the palace gardens.

A Royal Residence

THE FIRST KINGS OF SCOTLAND lived at Edinburgh Castle when in the city and enjoyed hunting in the area beneath what is now known as Arthur's Seat. Legend has it that when David I was out hunting he had a vision of a stag with a glowing cross (or rood) between its antlers. Interpreting this as a message from God, in 1128 he had an Augustinian abbey built on the spot where he had seen the stag and dedicated it to the Holy Rood. Others say that the name derives from a supposed fragment of the True Cross which had been brought to Scotland by David's mother, St Margaret.

The abbey flourished and was soon enlarged to include special apartments for use by the kings, who increasingly chose to stay there rather than in the exposed and far less comfortable castle. It was James IV, a gifted monarch and a great patron of the arts and sciences, who first converted the royal apartments at Holyroodhouse into a palace. Described by the scholar Erasmus as having 'wonderful powers of mind, an astonishing knowledge of everything, an unconquerable magnanimity and the most abundant generosity', James married Margaret Tudor, daughter of the English king Henry VII, in the abbey in 1503. This marriage is sometimes known as the Union of the Thistle and

RIGHT
David I's vision of a stag with a glowing cross between its antlers has become the symbol of Holyroodhouse. This carved stag is part of the fountain in the Forecourt.

BELOW LEFT
The nave of Holyrood Abbey in the spring sunshine.

BELOW RIGHT
James V, painted about 1550.

the Rose and was to have far-reaching consequences for the Stuart dynasty a century later when his great-grandson, James VI, was crowned James I of England.

Nothing survives of the early palace buildings, but it appears that they were laid out around a quadrangle, echoing the abbey buildings, a layout that has survived to this day. James IV's son, James V, built a fortified tower to provide new royal lodgings. This is the oldest surviving part of the palace today.

James V's daughter Mary was only six days old when she inherited the throne on her father's death in 1542. A great-granddaughter of Henry VII, the infant queen was next in line by blood to the English throne after Henry VIII's children. She was betrothed to Henry's son, the future Edward VI, but the treaty was breached by Scottish Catholics opposed to an agreement with the English king who had broken so decisively with Rome.

Furious, Henry VIII ordered a series of savage raids on Scotland, which became known as 'The Rough Wooing'. His army even attacked Holyrood Abbey but the Scots refused to give in to the English king. In 1548 Mary, Queen of Scots was betrothed instead to the Dauphin François, heir to the French king Henri II, and was sent to be brought up at the French court.

Mary was briefly Queen of France before her husband died in 1560. The following year she decided to return to Scotland in spite of the fact that the religious reforms led by John Knox meant that it was by then a Protestant country. At first she ruled successfully with the help of her advisers, but her disastrous marriage to Henry, Lord Darnley, in 1565 was to lead to tragedy.

ABOVE
Mary, Queen of Scots, about 1558, by François Clouet.

BELOW LEFT
Portrait of a Man known as David Rizzio, about 1620.

BELOW RIGHT
The Supper Room, where Mary, Queen of Scots was dining with her ladies on the night Rizzio was murdered.

ABOVE
A miniature of James VI
of Scotland and I of England
by Nicholas Hilliard,
inscribed 1614.

Darnley was a great-grandson of Henry VII and a member of the intensely ambitious Lennox family. He was little liked: spoilt and petulant, and easily manipulated by Mary's enemies, Darnley was bitterly jealous of Mary's relationship with her Italian secretary, David Rizzio. On 9 March 1566 he and a group of conspirators burst into the heavily pregnant queen's supper room at Holyroodhouse, dragged Rizzio to her outer chamber and stabbed him to death.

The relationship between the queen and Darnley never recovered. Their son, James, was born that summer but when Darnley was murdered the following February, many people suspected that Mary was involved. Her marriage only three months later to the Earl of Bothwell, generally believed to be responsible for Darnley's murder, sealed Mary's fate. Her Protestant Lords rose against her and forced her to abdicate in favour of her infant son, who became James VI. Fleeing to England in the hope that Elizabeth I would support her cause, Mary was instead kept captive for 19 years and was eventually executed at Fotheringay Castle on 8 February 1587.

Mary's son, James VI, Scotland's first Protestant king, was brought up in Stirling. From the age of 13 he lived at Holyroodhouse, where extensive improvements were carried out to accommodate a household that eventually numbered around 600 people. James's queen, Anne of Denmark, was crowned in the abbey in 1590, but after the death of Elizabeth I in 1603 and James's accession to the English throne as James I, the king and his court moved to London. Holyroodhouse was never to be a permanent court again.

RIGHT
The great east window at
the end of the nave of
Holyrood Abbey.

The palace and abbey were renovated in 1633 for the Scottish coronation of James's son, Charles I, but he did not stay long in Scotland. During the Civil War the palace was occupied by Cromwell's troops and largely abandoned after it was damaged extensively by fire in 1650.

The restoration of the monarchy in 1660 brought a change of fortune to Holyroodhouse after years of disuse. Keen to assert Edinburgh's role as a centre of royal government, the Scottish Privy Council ordered much of the palace to be rebuilt in the latest style of seventeenth-century courts. Designed by the Scottish architect Sir William Bruce, the new palace, like Charles II's remodelled Windsor Castle, incorporated a processional route through the king's apartments. The route took visitors through a series of increasingly sumptuously decorated rooms designed to impress with the power of the monarchy.

In spite of taking a great interest in his new palace, Charles II never stayed there. Instead, he appointed his brother James, Duke of York, the king's High Commissioner in Scotland. As a Roman Catholic, James was viewed with suspicion by many in England, but in 1679 and 1680 he and his second wife, Mary of Modena, took up residence at Holyroodhouse. The rebuilding work was not quite complete, but James brought his court with him and Holyroodhouse was once again used as a royal palace. Under James's patronage, culture flourished in Edinburgh.

James's first wife had been Protestant; they had two daughters, Mary and Anne. But Mary of Modena was a Catholic

ABOVE
Charles II, about 1670, by Sir Peter Lely.

BELOW LEFT
James II and Family, 1694, by Pierre Mignard. James is shown with his second wife, Queen Mary, and their children.

BELOW RIGHT
The Quadrangle was designed in classical style, with Doric, Ionic and Corinthian columns used in ascending order to reflect the status of each floor.

and when she gave birth to a son, James Francis Edward Stuart, Protestants in England and Scotland were alarmed at the prospect of a Catholic heir to the throne. When James succeeded his brother in 1685, as James VII of Scotland and James II of England, he converted the abbey church of Holyrood into a Roman Catholic Chapel Royal. Fears that he planned to reintroduce Catholicism eventually led to the 'Glorious Revolution' of 1688. Supported by the English nobles, the Protestant William of Orange landed in England to claim the throne on behalf of his wife – James's eldest daughter, Mary. James, his wife and son, James Francis Edward Stuart, were forced into exile in France, but he continued to maintain his claim to the throne until his death in 1701. His supporters, and those of his son, were known as Jacobites, from Jacobus, the Latin form of the name James.

The palace was left in the care of its hereditary Keepers, the dukes of Hamilton, who took over the queen's apartments in James V's Tower and lived there in great luxury. In 1707 the Act of Union united the kingdoms of Scotland and England, and the Scottish Parliament was dissolved. The Council Chamber at the palace became redundant and with no prospect of a visit from the sovereign, Holyroodhouse declined in importance, providing grace-and-favour apartments for members of the Scottish nobility.

Meanwhile, James's son, known as the Old Pretender, had inherited his father's claim to the throne. After a failed attempt to regain it in 1715, it was left to his son, the Young Pretender, popularly known as Bonnie Prince Charlie, to launch another

attempt to regain the crown for the Stuarts. When he landed on the west coast of Scotland in 1745, the Jacobite clans of the Highlands rose in his support and the prince was able to march through Scotland, seize Edinburgh and proclaim his father James VIII, King of Scots. Bonnie Prince Charlie was made Regent and he took up residence at Holyroodhouse, riding into the palace 'amidst the cries of 60,000 people, who fill'd the air with their acclamations of joy'.

For a short time Holyroodhouse was a court once more. The prince conducted official business in the palace and dined in public view, while the Great Gallery became the setting for a ball and other entertainments. But after six weeks Bonnie Prince Charlie left Edinburgh to continue his efforts to secure the throne. A final confrontation between the Jacobites and troops loyal to the Hanoverian king George II took place at the Battle of Culloden in April 1746. The rebellion was crushed, hopes of restoring a Catholic Stuart monarchy finally ended, and Bonnie Prince Charlie fled Scotland. He spent the rest of his life in exile on the Continent and died in 1788.

In 1822 George IV received a rapturous welcome when he arrived in Edinburgh. He was the first reigning monarch to visit Scotland for nearly 200 years. His itinerary was devised by the Scottish writer Sir Walter Scott, who played to the king's love of extravagance and pageantry by arranging a spectacular ceremony when George entered the palace as King of Scotland.

Holyroodhouse had for a number of years accommodated the comte d'Artois, brother of Louis XVI of France, and later Charles X,

ABOVE
Prince Charles Edward Stuart, 1739, by Louis Gabriel Blanchet. Grandson of James VII and II, Prince Charles was popularly known as Bonnie Prince Charlie or the Young Pretender.

BELOW
An Incident in the Rebellion of 1745, attributed to David Morier.

George IV, 1829, by
Sir David Wilkie. The king
wears Highland dress, made
for his visit to Scotland in
1822 by George Hunter of
Princes Street at a cost of
£1,354 18s.

in exile following the French Revolution, but the palace was in a poor state of repair. George IV stayed more comfortably at nearby Dalkeith Palace but some of the State Apartments were refurbished and redecorated so that he could host a number of receptions. A Great Drawing Room was created in Charles II's old Guard Chamber (now the Throne Room), which was hung with crimson cloth fringed with gold for the occasion. At the first reception, or levee, George IV wore full Highland dress 'in compliment to the country' to receive 1,200 gentlemen, many of whom had queued for hours to be presented. Later in the week, another reception was held at the palace for more than 400 ladies.

The king was shown around Mary, Queen of Scots' apartments by the Duke of Hamilton's housekeeper. He admired the State Bed, now in the King's Bedchamber, described by Sir Walter Scott as the 'couch of the Rose of Scotland'. In fact, the bed had been moved from the Duke of Hamilton's apartments and was made long after Mary's death, but George was impressed and decreed that 'in repairing the palace, these apartments should be preserved, sacred from every alteration'.

George IV's visit prompted a new interest in Scotland. His niece, Queen Victoria, also came north and first visited Edinburgh in 1842. 'We passed by Holyrood Chapel, which is old and full of interest', she wrote in her diary, describing the palace as 'a royal-looking old place'. Victoria was so delighted with Scotland – 'this most beautiful country which I am proud to call my own' – that she bought Balmoral Castle as a Highland retreat.

*Queen Victoria's Sitting-Room
or Morning Drawing Room*,
1863, by George M. Greig.
The principal rooms were
redecorated for Queen
Victoria, who used the Privy
Chamber as a drawing room.
The Jacob de Wet painting
above the mantelpiece was
thought unsuitable for ladies
and was covered with a mirror.

Its location made Holyroodhouse a convenient stop for the Queen and her family going to and from Balmoral, and their frequent visits restored the palace to its position as Scotland's foremost royal residence. The palace was completely renovated in 1850: the spectacular plasterwork ceilings in the State Apartments were cleaned and repainted in rich colours to complement the panelling and tapestries, and the furnishings supplemented with pieces sent up from Buckingham Palace. Later the apartments on the second floor were decorated with what the Queen described as 'pretty carpets and chintzes' as private apartments for the Royal Family.

Scotland continued to be popular with the Royal Family during the twentieth century and a number of improvements were carried out to make Holyroodhouse more comfortable. Central heating and electric light were installed for King George V's first visit with Queen Mary in 1911, while a programme of renovations after the First World War included new bedrooms, a lift and modernised kitchens. Holyroodhouse was recognised as the sovereign's official residence in Scotland, and the palace began to be used on a regular basis for garden parties and ceremonies such as investitures and presentations.

It continues to be a working palace today. Each year, Her Majesty The Queen spends a week at the palace for Royal Week, when she meets Scots from all walks of life on visits around Scotland, holds private audiences, receptions and investitures, and welcomes thousands of guests to Holyroodhouse at the annual Garden Party. Members of the Royal Family also use the palace to host events in support of charities and other organisations throughout the year.

ABOVE
The annual Ceremony of the Keys takes place on the palace Forecourt.

BELOW LEFT
Her Majesty The Queen holding an audience with Scotland's First Minister in the Presence Chamber, 2019.

BELOW RIGHT
HM Queen Elizabeth II, 2018, by Nicky Philipps. This portrait of Her Majesty The Queen was specially commissioned to hang at Holyroodhouse.

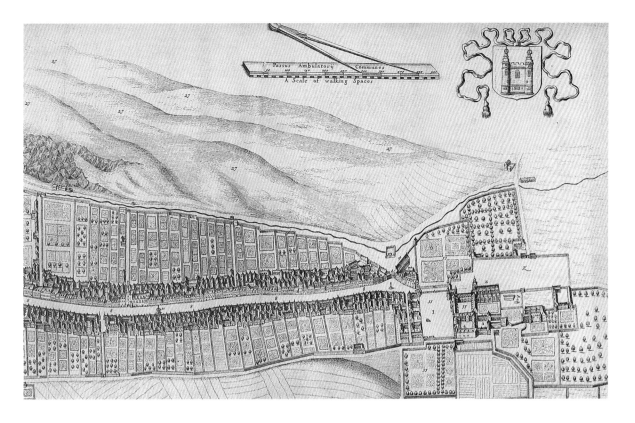

ABOVE
Plan of Holyroodhouse from a
bird's-eye view of Edinburgh,
1647.

BELOW
Prince Harry and Ms Meghan
Markle at Holyroodhouse to
host a reception for young
people before their wedding
in 2018.

At other times of the year, the palace is a popular visitor attraction. The Queen's Gallery was opened in 2002 to celebrate The Queen's Golden Jubilee and offers a rolling programme of exhibitions of works of art from the Royal Collection. Holyroodhouse itself has recently undergone a series of improvements, including the creation of a new Learning Centre and visitor facilities, refreshed displays of works of art from the Royal Collection and two new gardens for the public. These were all designed to improve the experience of visiting the palace and to reconnect it with the city.

A Tour of Holyroodhouse: Forecourt and Quadrangle

THE SYMMETRICAL FAÇADE that greets the visitor crossing the Forecourt looks very much as it did when Holyroodhouse was remodelled for Charles II in the 1670s. The oldest part of the palace is the massive tower on the left, built by James V in 1528 and originally fortified with a drawbridge and moat to make the royal lodgings secure. The tower on the right was added in the seventeenth century to balance the appearance of the façade.

The Forecourt is dominated by the magnificent fountain, installed by Queen Victoria and Prince Albert in 1859. At the start of The Queen's summer visit to the palace for Royal Week, the Forecourt is a parade ground for the Ceremony of the Keys, when the Lord Provost welcomes Her Majesty into the city of Edinburgh, 'your ancient and hereditary kingdom of Scotland', and presents her with the keys to the city.

Inside, the palace is built around a central Quadrangle. The cloister-like layout echoes the monastic origins of the palace and was redesigned in a grand classical style by Sir William Bruce when Holyroodhouse was rebuilt for Charles II.

ABOVE
The Ceremony of the Keys.

RIGHT
The palace façade remains little changed since the seventeenth century, when the palace was remodelled for Charles II by Sir William Bruce.

The Quadrangle is laid out like a cloister, reflecting the monastic origins of the palace.

LEFT
Based on James V's fountain at Linlithgow Palace the fountain in the Forecourt shows figures enjoying typical aristocratic pursuits of the sixteenth century, such as hunting and music-making.

Great Stair

THIS IMPOSING STONE staircase was designed for Charles II as the first stage in a processional route that led through ever more elaborately decorated rooms towards the king. Built using the latest technology of the time, which enabled the steps to be cantilevered out from a single support at one end, the Great Stair was intended to impress the visitor from the start.

The spectacular plasterwork ceiling was the first in a series of increasingly ornate plasterwork creations that originally decorated the rooms along the processional route. The decoration, built up on a timber framework, was created in moulds from plaster reinforced with horsehair, and applied and finished by hand. In the corners, life-size figures of angels bear the symbols of kingship that form the Honours of Scotland: the crown, the sceptre and the sword.

At the bottom of the Great Stair hangs Sir David Wilkie's painting of George IV being presented with the keys to the Palace of Holyroodhouse by the hereditary Keeper, Alexander, 10th Duke of Hamilton. George IV was the first reigning monarch to visit Scotland since Charles I.

RIGHT
The Great Stair is decorated with fragments of Renaissance frescos purchased by Prince Albert, who also sent the sixteenth-century tapestries, from a series called *The Planets*, to Holyroodhouse in 1860.

Detail of plasterwork in the ceiling above the Great Stair. An angel holds the Scottish crown.

BELOW LEFT
The Queen and Pope Benedict XVI on the Great Stair during the Pope's State Visit in 2010.

BELOW RIGHT
The Entrance of George IV at Holyroodhouse, 1822–30, by Sir David Wilkie.

Royal Dining Room

ORIGINALLY THE GUARD CHAMBER used by soldiers charged with guarding access to the queen's apartments, this room was completely refurbished around 1800 for the Duke of Hamilton, Keeper of the Palace in the absence of the monarch. It was first used as a dining room at the end of Queen Victoria's reign and today is used by The Queen and other members of the Royal Family to entertain guests and to host dinners for Scottish charities and organisations of which they are patrons.

The eighteenth-century mahogany table is laid with pieces from a dessert service ordered by Queen Victoria. The silver on display is part of a service presented by Sir Alexander Grant to mark the Silver Jubilee of King George V in 1935 and was commissioned specifically for use at Holyroodhouse. Each of the more than 3,000 pieces in the service is hand-engraved with the Scottish Royal Crest. It includes everything from candelabra to cutlery, soufflé dishes to sauceboats, and teapots to asparagus tongs, and is so large that two service rooms are required to store and clean it. The gift also included damask table linen, which, like the silver, is still in use today.

ABOVE
Curtain detail.

RIGHT
The dining table laid with some of the magnificent silver service commissioned to mark the Silver Jubilee of King George V.

When used for dinners hosted by members of the Royal Family, every place is precisely set.

LEFT
Detail of crown and thistle plasterwork below the chimneypiece in the Royal Dining Room.

Throne Room

ORIGINALLY THE KING'S Guard Chamber, this room was transformed into a Great Drawing Room for George IV's visit in 1822. Hung with crimson cloth and equipped with a throne and canopy transported from Buckingham Palace, this was where George IV received Scottish gentlemen, some of whom queued for hours to be presented to him at a special levee that was organised to mark the first visit of a reigning monarch to Scotland in nearly 200 years. Ladies were invited to a separate reception called a Drawing Room.

The Throne Room was refurbished in 1927, when it was panelled with oak and given a new ceiling in the style of the seventeenth century. Today it continues to be used by members of the Royal Family for receptions and other events. It is hung with portraits of the Stuart kings and their consorts, most notably the powerful painting of Charles II by John Michael Wright. Although Charles never visited Holyroodhouse, he took a close interest in its rebuilding and is responsible in large part for the palace that we see today.

ABOVE
Charles II's queen, Catherine of Braganza, painted by Sir Peter Lely about 1663–5.

RIGHT
The Throne Room.

Upholstered throne chairs made for King George V and Queen Mary in 1911.

LEFT
Charles II, about 1671–6, by John Michael Wright.

Presence Chamber

JAMES, DUKE OF YORK and later James VII and II, was appointed the king's High Commissioner in Scotland by his brother Charles II in 1679. As representative of the king, James held court at Holyroodhouse and used this and the other State Apartments for their original purpose. The rooms were designed not only to control access but also to impress and intimidate visitors with the magnificence of the monarchy.

Today the Presence Chamber is used for receptions and audiences, but at James's court this was where visitors would wait in the hope of speaking to him. James's portrait hangs in the room together with those of his first wife, Anne Hyde, and of the Catholic Mary of Modena, whom he married after Anne's death. James's daughter, the future Queen Anne, stayed at the palace as a young girl and the Presence Chamber also contains a portrait of her, painted when she was a child.

When Queen Victoria was in residence, the room was used as a drawing room for the court. The four tapestries on the walls were sent up from Buckingham Palace in 1851 to make the room more comfortable. Made in Brussels in the mid-eighteenth century, two of the tapestries, *Asia* and *Africa*, are from a series called *The Four Continents*. The other two depict scenes from peasant life, one in a fish market and the other in a vegetable market where turnips, cabbages, asparagus and chard are for sale.

ABOVE
Queen Anne when a Child, about 1667–8, by Sir Peter Lely.

RIGHT
James VII and II when Duke of York, about 1665, by Sir Peter Lely.

LEFT
The Presence Chamber.

Privy Chamber

IN THE SEVENTEENTH CENTURY, only the most privileged of visitors would have been allowed from the Presence Chamber into the Privy Chamber to meet the king or his representative. The room's exclusive status is reflected in the sumptuous decoration and its view out over the gardens. The ornate ceiling is decorated with cherubs and eagles bearing the cipher of Charles II and the Honours of Scotland, while the central panels feature heraldic lions and unicorns.

The elaborately carved overmantel encloses a painting by the Dutch artist Jacob de Wet. His depiction of a reclining naked female being fed by an equally naked male was deemed unsuitable by the Victorians, and so was covered by a mirror when Queen Victoria used the room as her private drawing room. At the same time, the ceiling was painted in rich colours to complement the tapestries that have been hanging in Holyroodhouse since the seventeenth century. Queen Mary disliked the result and had it painted white during the 1911 renovations.

Today the room has reverted to its original purpose and is where The Queen gives private audiences to the First Minister of Scotland and visiting dignitaries.

ABOVE
Ceiling detail showing cherubs bearing the cipher of Charles II.

RIGHT
The Privy Chamber.

Detail of the card table depicting a three-handed card game laid out.

LEFT
Her Majesty watches a performance by the Royal Scottish Country Dance Society in the Privy Chamber.

King's Ante-Chamber

ONCE A WAITING ROOM for the King's Bedchamber, the Ante-Chamber enjoys fine views over the gardens and in 1850 served as Queen Victoria's bedroom. A hidden door at the back of the room leads into a dressing room and the suite of service rooms that runs behind the State Rooms and overlooks the Quadrangle.

The harpsicord, gilded and decorated with birds and foliage, bears an inscription that claims it was made in Antwerp in 1636 by Johannes Rucker, a famous maker of early keyboard instruments. However, it is now thought that the inscription was added later to increase its value.

The eighteenth-century harp was made in Paris and was bought for Holyroodhouse in 1931, at a cost of £17 10s, with an additional £4 10s paid to string it.

King's Bedchamber and King's Closet

IN THE SEVENTEENTH-CENTURY court the King's Bedchamber was a formal apartment where the king met advisers and discussed confidential matters of state. The room was used for levees, the ritual of dressing and undressing the king in the presence of his nobles, and only the most powerful members of court were allowed into such an intimate space. If Charles II had ever visited Holyroodhouse, he would probably have slept in more comfort elsewhere.

The room is dominated by the State Bed. An inventory of 1684 records the bed in the Duke of Hamilton's apartments in the palace but in the nineteenth century it was displayed in Mary, Queen of Scots' Bedchamber, where it became wrongly known as 'the couch of the Rose of Scotland'. The bed was later moved to the King's Bedchamber, restored and rehung with red damask to match the original fabric.

The King's Closet next door is a smaller, more intimate room, intended to be used as a private study by the king. In 1850 it became Queen Victoria's breakfast room and was hung with green and gold flock wallpaper.

ABOVE
Detail of the overmantel carving in the King's Closet.

RIGHT
The State Bed, 1675–1700, was probably made for Anne, Duchess of Hamilton. The most important room in the palace, the richly decorated King's Bedchamber marks the climax of the processional route through the State Apartments.

LEFT
The Apotheosis of Hercules, 1675, by Jacob de Wet.

A TOUR OF HOLYROODHOUSE

Great Gallery

THE DUTCH ARTIST Jacob de Wet was commissioned to paint the portraits of legendary and real Scottish kings that still hang in the Great Gallery. De Wet was contracted to paint 110 portraits, from Fergus I in 330 BC to Charles II, over a two-year period between 1684 and 1686, averaging one portrait a week. He was paid £120 a year for the work, and an additional £30 to paint the new king, James VII, after Charles II's death. Although the paintings are of variable quality and the likenesses of the earlier kings inevitably invented, the portraits in the Great Gallery symbolise the power of a dynasty stretching back nearly 2,000 years.

The Gallery has been used for a variety of purposes over the years. After the Union of Parliaments in 1707, Scottish peers gathered in the Great Gallery to elect a delegation to attend Parliament in Westminster. Bonnie Prince Charlie was said to have held a ball for his supporters there and King George V used it as the State Dining Room. It is still used for state banquets, dinners and receptions today as well as for investitures, when honours are awarded in recognition of outstanding achievements, personal bravery and service to the country.

ABOVE
Macbeth, as imagined by Jacob de Wet.

RIGHT
The Great Gallery.

The portraits in the Great Gallery are all by Jacob de Wet, who was commissioned to paint all the 'Kings who have Reigned over this Kingdome of Scotland'. Mary, Queen of Scots is the only woman represented.

LEFT
The Thistle Star, c.1893, part of the insignia of the Most Ancient and Most Noble Order of the Thistle. The highest order of chivalry in Scotland, the Order of the Thistle was established by James VII and II in 1687.

Lobby, Ante-Chamber and Lord Darnley's Bedchamber

THE LOBBY AND the Ante-Chamber lead into James V's Tower, the oldest surviving part of the palace, and to the room that was once Lord Darnley's Bedchamber. It was from this room that Lord Darnley reputedly made his way up the stairs to murder David Rizzio in Mary, Queen of Scots' apartments above.

These rooms were used by Bonnie Prince Charlie 200 years later, when he led a rebellion to regain the throne for the Stuarts. After landing in Scotland in 1745, the prince seized Edinburgh and set up court at Holyroodhouse, dining in the Ante-Chamber and meeting with his council in Lord Darnley's Bedchamber. The room now contains the richly decorated tester bed known as the Darnley Bed, although it was in fact made for the Duke of Hamilton in 1682. The prince reputedly slept in this bed, which was then in another part of the palace, during his stay.

After six weeks in Holyroodhouse, the prince marched to England with his troops, but the palace was ransacked by government soldiers after his departure. A Jacobite lady lamented that they 'destroy'd the apartment the Prince was in, tore down the silk bed he lay in, broke and carried off all the fine gilded glasses, cabinets and everything else'. In 1746 Bonnie Prince Charlie and the Jacobites were defeated at Culloden by the Hanoverian army led by the Duke of Cumberland, who stayed at Holyroodhouse and supposedly slept in the same bed the night before the battle.

ABOVE
Detail of the embroidered bedcover on the Darnley Bed, about 1700.

RIGHT
Henry Stewart, Lord Darnley and his brother Charles Stewart, Earl of Lennox, 1563, by Hans Eworth.

FAR LEFT
Lord Darnley climbed these stairs before dragging David Rizzio from Mary, Queen of Scots' Supper Room above and murdering him.

LEFT
Seventeenth-century jar flanked by two eighteenth-century vases in the Ante-Chamber.

Mary, Queen of Scots' Apartments

AFTER HER RETURN to Scotland in 1561, Mary, Queen of Scots occupied the rooms on the second floor of James V's Tower. She had a private Supper Room in the turret off her bedchamber and received official visitors in the Outer Chamber, a room that witnessed her encounters with John Knox, the indomitable Protestant reformer who openly condemned the queen for hearing mass, dancing and wearing fashionable clothes.

In 1565 Mary married Henry, Lord Darnley, but the marriage was an unhappy one and Darnley was deeply jealous of her relationship with her secretary, David Rizzio. On 9 March 1566, a heavily pregnant Mary was dining with her ladies and Rizzio in the Supper Room when Darnley burst in. Rizzio clung to the queen's skirts but Darnley ignored the queen's horrified protests, dragging her secretary out of the Supper Room, across the Bedchamber and on to the Outer Chamber. It was there that Darnley and his co-conspirators murdered Rizzio, stabbing him 56 times in a brutal attack that was said to have left a bloodstain on the floorboards well into the eighteenth century, when the Duke of Hamilton's servants recounted the story in gruesome detail to fascinated visitors.

RIGHT
Queen Mary's Bed Chamber, after George M. Greig. The apartments were a popular visitor attraction in the nineteenth century. Note the tester bed, now in the King's Bedchamber.

The Outer Chamber, with the display cases containing the Stuart Relics.

BELOW LEFT
Mary, Queen of Scots, about 1559–61, by François Clouet. The portrait shows the queen in mourning for three members of her family in France.

BELOW RIGHT
The modern crewel-work bedhangings follow a seventeenth-century Scottish design.

Abbey Ruins and Gardens

VISITORS LEAVE THE palace through the ruins of Holyrood Abbey, founded in 1128 by David I. The foundation flourished but the monastic buildings were abandoned after the Reformation and the abbey left badly damaged. The nave was renovated for the Scottish coronation of Charles I in 1633, and refitted as the Chapel Royal during the reign of James VII and II, but it was ransacked by an Edinburgh mob in 1688 and eventually fell into ruin. Today the nave is all that remains of the abbey church that once witnessed royal coronations, weddings and burials.

The gardens surrounding the palace have seen many changes over the years. In the sixteenth century there were areas for jousting and archery, and there may have been a tennis court, as well as a walled Privy Garden. The knot gardens, fashionable in the seventeenth century, were replaced by a Physic Garden. However, by the time Queen Victoria came to Holyroodhouse, the grounds were overgrown and Prince Albert enthusiastically took charge of redeveloping the palace's surroundings. Since then the gardens have continued to be improved, most recently by the creation of the new Physic Garden, inspired by historical records.

RIGHT
The east end of the ruined abbey church.

Artist's impression of the new Physic Garden.

OVERLEAF
The Highlanders, 4th Battalion, Royal Regiment of Scotland, form a Guard of Honour on the Forecourt.

BELOW LEFT
During Royal Week, Her Majesty The Queen invites 8,000 people from all walks of life to enjoy the gardens at the annual Garden Party.

BELOW RIGHT
The Abbey fell into ruins in the eighteenth century.

Highlights of the Collection at Holyroodhouse

THE DARNLEY JEWEL OR LENNOX JEWEL

One of the most important early jewels in the Royal Collection, this spectacular piece was probably made for Lady Margaret Douglas, Countess of Lennox, following the death of her husband Matthew Stewart, Earl of Lennox and Regent of Scotland, in 1571. Margaret centred the family's ambitions on her grandson, James, Darnley's son with Mary, Queen of Scots, who later became James VI of Scotland and James I of England.

The heart-shaped jewel is made from coloured enamels, rubies, blue glass and an emerald. Intended to be worn around the neck or on the breast, it is elaborately decorated with complex symbols and inscriptions, some of which – such as 'QVHA. HOPIS. STIL. CONSTANLY. VITH PATIENCE SAL. OBTEAIN. VICTORIE. IN YAIR. PRETENCE' ('who hopes still constantly with patience shall obtain victory in their claim') – may have been written with James in mind.

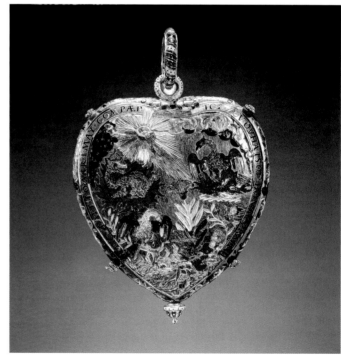

SILVER-GILT POMANDER

This pomander, made about 1550, is said to have belonged to Mary, Queen of Scots. Originally designed to hold a ball of aromatic spices or herbs to ward off infections and noxious smells, during the Middle Ages pomanders were worn suspended from the neck or a girdle, and when decorated or enriched with gems were carried as decorative objects. By the sixteenth century pomanders were divided into segments, each of which could be filled with a different powdered spice.

'A CATTE'

Mary, Queen of Scots was a skilled needlewoman. Held captive in England by the Earl of Shrewsbury between 1569 and 1584, she spent much of her time embroidering with Shrewsbury's wife, Elizabeth (Bess of Hardwick). Together they devised embroideries as small panels of canvas work that could be worked easily in coloured silk threads on a portable frame. The canvas panels were drawn out by an embroiderer, outlined in black silk and then completed by the queen or the countess.

This embroidered panel depicts a ginger cat with a mouse on a chequered floor, and bears Mary's cipher. The Queen of Scots was kept prisoner for 19 years on the orders of her famously red-headed English cousin, so it is possible that Mary was alluding to herself as the mouse here, and Elizabeth I as the cat.

PARURE OF NECKLACE, BROOCH AND EARRINGS

A parure is a set of jewellery intended to be worn together. This set was created at different times but the brooch and parts of the necklace date to the sixteenth century. They were said to have been given by Mary, Queen of Scots to Mary Seton, a devoted attendant and friend who shared many years of her exile. She was an excellent hairdresser whose services the queen greatly admired. The gold and white enamel brooch is the oldest part of the parure and is set with four pearls and a central ruby in a box setting. The necklace is made of gold and enamel, set with pearls, emeralds and rubies. The earrings were created in the nineteenth century.

The parure passed to Mary Seton's descendants until it was sold and presented to Queen Mary on the occasion of King George V's Silver Jubilee in May 1935.

THE HOLYROOD ORDINAL

An ordinal is a book of rules for the daily services throughout the year in an abbey or church. It provides information for the adaptation of services and lessons for special days, such as feast days and saints' days. This manuscript dates from the mid-fifteenth century and was written specifically for the Augustinian abbey of Holyrood, founded by David I in 1128. It was used at the daily meeting of the Chapter, held in the Chapter House, when a brief record was read of the saints connected with the day; a chapter of the rule was also read or, on Sundays and festivals, the appointed gospel with its homily. The Chapter then moved on to the business of the day, such as the assignment of work to different persons, the hearing of complaints and the administration of discipline.

ENCHANTED POOL BOWL

Inspired by the River Dee, which runs through the Balmoral estate, the bowl represents a pool, with freshwater pearls and bulrushes made of silver gilt. It was presented to The Queen by the Edinburgh jewellers Hamilton & Inches in 2016 to mark her 90th birthday and the 150th anniversary of the company.

TAPESTRY: *APOLLO AND DIANA SLAYING THE CHILDREN OF NIOBE*

The Palace of Holyroodhouse has an exceptional collection of tapestries. In earlier centuries tapestries were high-status items, adding colour and warmth to rooms, and were displayed only when the monarch was in residence. An inventory compiled after the death of Charles II in 1685 recorded two sets of tapestries that are still hanging at the palace, one of which was the series depicting the 'History of Diana', described as 'Ane sute of Fyne Bruxells hingings containing seven piece wherein is described the history of Diana' and now on display in the King's Ante-Chamber and the Privy Chamber.

This panel depicts Apollo and Diana slaying the children of Niobe. In classical mythology, Niobe was the mother of six sons and six daughters. She boasted about the number of her children to Latona, mother to only one son, Apollo, and one daughter, Diana, who both punished Niobe for her pride by killing all her children.

CHINESE PUNCH BOWL

Made in China about 1765, this porcelain bowl is painted on either side with the royal coat of arms of Scotland. In between appear the Star and Badge of the Order of the Thistle. This may mean that the bowl was presented to the Order, but it is also possible that it was made for a Jacobite club. These were male-only associations that sprang up across the country after the 1715 risings. They met secretly in inns, alehouses and taverns to honour the exiled Stuarts by singing seditious songs, collecting for the cause or recruiting for rebellion. On these occasions a toast would be made to 'the king over the water' in reference to the man they considered their rightful monarch, who was in exile overseas. For the toast, glasses were passed over a vessel containing water such as a finger bowl to symbolise the voyage between Scotland and the Continent.

TUREEN

This maiolica tureen was made in Italy in the second half of the eighteenth century. It is painted with the arms of Henry Benedict Stuart, the last heir of the Jacobite line. Made Duke of York in the Jacobite peerage by his father, James Francis Edward Stuart (the Old Pretender), Henry spent his career in the Roman Catholic Church and rose to become a cardinal. On the death of his brother, Charles Edward Stuart, commonly known as Bonnie Prince Charlie, the Jacobites called him Henry I of Scotland and IX of England and Ireland, but he referred to himself as Cardinal York.

The tureen is painted with his coat of arms and his cardinal's hat, surrounded by floral sprays and scattered insects. It was bequeathed to George III after Henry's death in 1807, and has recently undergone conservation by the Royal Collection.

DIRK, SCABBARD, KNIFE AND FORK

George IV visited Scotland in 1822, the first reigning monarch to do so for nearly 200 years. Encouraged by the novelist Sir Walter Scott, he ordered full Highland dress, with accoutrements, from George Hunter of Princes Street, Edinburgh, which he wore at his levee at the palace 'in compliment to the country'. Among other items, Hunter supplied the dirk, scabbard, knife and fork on display. A dirk is a stabbing knife originally used for hunting and for close-quarter fighting, while the knife and fork hark back to earlier centuries when people carried their own eating implements. Traditionally, affluent Highlanders kept a knife – and fork once the use of forks became more widespread in the eighteenth century – in a sheath with a dirk. Later these became mainly decorative additions to Highland dress.